I0133490

1

The highest excellence in martial arts is not the victory in a hundred battles-but to defeat the enemy without fighting

Sun Tzu

Word of caution!

A Book about martial arts can never substitute professionel instruction! Do not attempt any of the techniques described in this work without the supervision of a qualified instructor.

The Author disclaims any legal liability in case of misuse of the information given in this book!

With this advice in mind-read on.

© By Mudo Nandayo 2011 all rights reserved

The author wishes to thank the following persons for their contribution to the present work:

Christophe Huber-photographer

Ivan Hippolyte-location host

Sigrid de Schwartz-photographs

Natascha B. Hakula-advisor

He also wishes to thank the following persons for the influence, support, kindness and effort they bestowed on him during his martial arts training and career. In the chronological order as they came into his life:

Shifu Ferdinand Wondrak	Inyo Do
Sensei A. Wondrak	Sip Sun Do/Kickboxing
Master R. D. Gomez	Sip Sun Do/Arnis
Master Viktor Krueger	Shoot-wrestling/MMA
Sensei Ivan Hippolyte	Muay Thai Boxing
Sensei Ernesto Hoost	Muay Thai Boxing
Sensei H. Ditmars	Iu Ryu Jujutsu
Master Frans Stroeven	JKD/ Escrima/WKFS
Master Koos Cuijpers	Krav Maga/WKFS

TABLE OF CONTENT

INYO BUDO & TAIJUJTSU

The term Taijutsu does not necessarily denote a specific martial art like Jujutsu-which is mostly associated with grappling and joint locks, especially since the appearance of Gracie Brazilian Jujutsu and the globalization of a Form of Full contact sport and cross training, simply called MMA-mixed martial arts. However, there are several different martial arts schools or systems especially in Japan, referring to their art as Taijutsu, the term translating as "full body art or principle", which are totally different in character and approach.

Ninjutsu's Bujinkan Taijutsu for example, is a composite system of unarmed striking, kicking, grappling and the use and disarming of a variety of weapons, like sword, dagger and staff.

The Taijutsu of the Shosho School however, uses mainly striking and kicking, but has no or very little grappling in its curriculum.

Inyo Taijutsu, the way I see it, has not really fixed methods or techniques; rather the use and adaptability of the entire body under the aspect of the governing dynamics of neutral, complementary and antagonistic forces or energies, which are at work in any given situation. In terms of body movements, as well as principal approach. A number of certain basic natural body movements are the foundation, on which every move and response is build upon. But again, freedom of movement and choice is the primary concern.

Be it in exercising with weights or bodyweight, in moving and even standing and walking, the perception of the antagonistic and supporting muscles, tendons and joints at work at any given moment-that is Taijutsu, too. The awareness and basic knowledge of the human body - also your own, its anatomy and physiology, is of vital importance for understanding oneself and maximizing one's own potential.

 To use the whole body as a single harmonious, united entity, originally designed for perception and movement, relating to its environment as an effective tool of survival-that is Taijutsu in its widest sense or purest form-depending on ones personal perception.

Word of caution: Any of the examples in this book, depicting protective responses-"techniques", are merely suggestive and by no means represent a fixed pattern or standard or "usual" way of doing things.

THE TRINITY OF INYO - BUDO & TAIJUTSU

FITNESS - SELF PROTECTION - PERSONAL DEVELOPMENT

INYO- balancing the governing dynamics

To know what works in any situation supportive (+) - what is antagonistic (-) - and how to find a balance between them. Mastering the governing dynamics principle allows one to adjust easier to the changes in daily life.

BUDO-the spiritual and martial way of life

The path - a quest for answers, or for a peaceful life, ones own personal cause or philosophy-whatever gives meaning to your life- - karma in the widest sense.

(Cause-effect-consequence)

TAIJUTSU-the full body principle

The principle of the whole body-used as a survival tool and vehicle to a higher consciousness; thru keeping fit, healthy and well conditioned, using ones self protection skills only in real emergencies without unnecessary boasting or brutality and violence.

GOVERNING DYNAMICS

The shortest, fastest and most direct route to connect any two points is a straight line. The opposite of a straight line is a circle. The third way of moving is a triangle, a conjunction of straight line and circle. The inside of a circle is a cross. This is the geometry of movement. Counter a straight move with a circular one, move forward, backward and left and right in a cross, to attack, intercept, counter and evade. Use a triangular and circular move to surround your opponent, a half turn to let him pass you by. Attack and defend in a 360° angle. Use only body natural movements and move as a single, harmonious unit of energy transmission. To be and not to be-that is the answer, think of that! Cause-effect-consequence!

Inyo Budo was designed by the ancient Taoists to transcend the notion of martial art "styles" into energy and movement expressed thru the whole body, without labeling it as the property of a certain artificial tradition. Human being moving and thinking in action is always behind any martial concept, no matter what name it has been given.

This brings us to the main issue: what is INYO BUDO and what is it not, which in itself speaks for the characteristic of the philosophy and theory behind the concept.

TO BE AND NOT TO BE IS THE ANSWER to many fundamental questions. It's a matter of perspective. (Cause-effect-consequence)

INYO BUDO is rather the spiritual and TAIJUTSU the physical embodiment of the yin yang principle, following the idea of self protection and self improvement, using the whole body. The term merely denotes the characteristic of the spiritual source; it is not a fixed label. It only points out the direction or purpose. Inyo Budo is NOT a Ryu or school - it is an idea, a spiritual outlook or concept with a physical basis: the yin yang principle and use of the whole body. Self protection and self improvement-that's all!

The purpose of real Budo is not just combat efficiency, also the spiritual and psycho-physical well being of its exponents. Again, Self-protection and self improvement is the goal!

Inyo Budo has the use of a minimum effort-maximum protective efficiency as its top priority and core principle. That means to do the least, while getting out the most, with the best possible protection of one self. Being like water, the attack is neutralizing absorbed by the fluent energy of the physical response; giving in-to redirect the opponent's energy and force against them.

Taijutsu is the art of using the human anatomy, physiology and the principle of minimum effort-maximum efficiency to protect oneself or others from any possible attack, armed or unarmed. The whole body is used as weapon and target of protection. This means of course a responsibility of caution and humility that comes with the power and skill of martial arts.

It is nothing else than the meaning and expression of using the whole body to protect and improve. The concept of natural totality is the key principle to understand the constant interchange of the antagonistic-complementary and neutral energies of yin yang (IN-YO) - or as we now call them- GOVERNING DYNAMICS!

THERE IS NO MARTIAL ART CALLED INYO BUDO TAIJUTSU, it's just an indication of the concept behind the way! NEITHER IS THERE A FOUNDER CALLED MUDO NANDAYO! These are just footnotes on your path.

The principal moves and theories of energy transmission and release are so compatible, that they complete each other; this is the law of harmonious energy incorporation. Natural body movements

14

enhance and complement one another and ensure a fluent, revolving linking of movements and energy fluctuation.

Relaxed, fast and powerful moves and reactions- that is the result of the correct execution of harmonious interchange of the governing body mechanics, in conjunction with the factors timing, balance and distance. Well, having precision in ones move actually does hurt-your opponent, so you better be as accurate as possible.

In other words, stick to the basics, using correct posture, breathing, guard closed and poised; a stable but flexible stance, relaxed but ready to explode in any direction with any part of the body, moving like an eight legged beast. With the ferocity of a slightly wounded tiger and the venomous speed of a cobra in irritation, you're vision peripheral and your mind calm, sense the right moment and distance to respond quickly, not in a hurry. Aim well. Neutralize the attack instantly and finish the confrontation with the calmness and precision of an eagle, using leverage and gravity. That is the core of Inyo Budo.

Life is a spiritual practice, not the other way around. A martial artist is a man of reason, of benevolence, not violence and ego tripping. Don't break what you can't fix. Destruction is easy-healing is difficult, a true martial artist is both, warrior and healer. The purpose of Inyo Budo is to help one self and others to enhance and improve life's quality and the understanding of oneself and nature.

The protective part is also just a tool to be able to live one's life without those mental restrictions caused by anxiety and ignorance. Working on ones improvement is one of the noblest character traits a human being can have. Also one of the hardest battles ever fought! Improving oneself means confronting the worst enemy: inside oneself!

Taijutsu's main objective is to keep the exponent safe and alive, but BUDO's ultimate goal is to reduce violence in the world, to help people change for the better and to unite mankind in harmony. It is a movement, a spiritual philosophy and concept, rather than a combat oriented, fixed patterned form of "self defense". Self protection starts with one's attitude and awareness. Weapons are tools of ill omen and Fighting methods are the worst way to solve a conflict, therefore, they must be sound and effective and only be used in case of a real emergency. Never for crooked, selfish purposes. This will always backfire. (Karma)! That's the principle of cause-effect and consequence; a detail that is often conveniently forgotten or left out when quoting the Buddhist carmic logic of causality. There is a fine line between spirituality and madness.

Human being is a strange, inquisitive, violent and (self)destructive creature-at its worst; a beauty minded, kind, compassionate, creative species, trying to understand its own origin and essence and the Universe it believes to exist in – at its best. The only living being on Earth, able to safe other species from extinction, while having the sinister power to destroy itself and its own planet. Why do human beings keep attacking and killing their own kind? Can You Dig It?

The study and mastery of martial arts is a noble, life long endeavor, but the path of a spiritual warrior has neither beginning nor end. It is an endless process of dynamics; realizing, distilling, and embodying the physical and spiritual principles in action and stillness.

This does not mean picking and collecting random techniques, or following a single, fixed, unchangeable doctrine, or way of doing and perceiving things, it means distilling and analyzing certain principles, fusing them, leading to the modification and creation of certain moves, which can be building blocks for other moves and principles.

Therefore, anyone interested in learning martial arts should know that it is not about fighting or defeating others, it is about overcoming ones ego, ones own inner enemy. The violent will not come to a good end; neither does the greedy one or the liar, who lies to himself as much as to others. Try to find a balance between the antagonistic and the complementary. When both forces are equal, they nullify each other. This is a state of equilibrium. If one dynamic predominates, it will reach its maximum potential and turn into its opposite quality; the same process is repeated continually with the forces of antagonism and support, called in Chinese YIN YANG- in Japanese IN YO- in the west we call them simply GOVERNING DYNAMICS- a more generic and scientific term, originated by the Nobel price awarded mathematician, Professor John F. Nash.

This is the key to understand human nature, the principles of the Universe and the spirit of martial arts. This is the Tao of INYO BUDO. It is designed as a way to improve the quality of ones life, not to defeat the enemy in battles not obliged to fight. The practice of using the human anatomy and physiology to hurt or even kill others has been much dramatized and mystified over the last 2500 years. The invention of myriads of "fighting styles", "combat methods", "schools" and "systems" has led to many rivalries among exponents of all the different fractions, misunderstandings about martial arts, the power of human spirit and physique as well as the moral aspect of violence and warfare itself.

In other words, if you copy and limit yourself, you will never be able to explore and apply your full potential. Don't fool yourself into thinking you're perfect, you're a master. This is the beginning of defeat, driven by the ego of complacency and ignorance. A great master was a great student before he was allowed to teach. Because he was open to learning and improving, he reached a certain level, but when the ego sets in, growth stops and the ego's satisfaction will be pursued.

That is the beginning of madness. Fulfillment of the egos needs. That's the real meaning of the old cliché "rid your self of desires". It does not mean stop desiring nice clothes, a passionate, romantic love affair or delicious food; it means to realize the difference between wishful thinking and real purpose. You can enjoy all that is, but don't indulge in it and get lost in the pursuit of shallow satisfaction of the senses, leading in the end to more suffering. Don't force things, go with the flow. Take care of your self and those who need you, for as a martial artist, as an instructor, you are a sage, a healer, a teacher and gentleman ; in short, someone to respect and look up to, some one that makes you feel good being around.

That is the influence you should desire, by living the good example. No one expects you to be a holy man, just to be your self. Sincerely, honest and kind, those are the qualities of a decent martial artist, not bragging, intimidating, downgrading other masters and arts or prostituting the art one represents.

No martial art was ever invented for the sole purpose of killing or committing violence- the true martial artist fights only when his life or that of others is at stake, never for vain glory, his ego or to respond to insults by ignorant people of no account. That does not mean you have to take all the shit people wonna download on you, react-if at all, appropriately to your situation, keeping in mind the evolution of any situation: CAUSE-EFFECT-CONSEQUENCE!

" You must defeat yourself first, than you can try to subdue someone else". In Chin Na the phrase,"before you can control someone else, control yourself first", applies to handling a physical and emotional state of being. The Universe teaches in myriads of ways, some more direct, others more elusive, but the fact that we all learn from every moment in life, makes it what it is: a spiritual quest. Throughout life one witnesses it's up's and downs, facing and experiencing conflicts; physically, verbally, and otherwise, as well as social ignorance and ego tripping-that's the way of the world. See it as a spiritual practice. Surrender to it.

Life is full of obstacles, draw backs, tragedies and injustice all around us. Well, ups and downs are just the manifestation of the bipolar energies of plus and minus; INYO - antagonistic and supportive. Meditate on that. Nothing lasts forever, any condition, good or bad will diminish and pass and recur like the 4 seasons or day and night -those are the natural cycles. Inyo and Kyo-jitsu- balance as well as excess and deficiency. This is another easily verifiable Universal law everything on Earth abides by. Inyo Budo is concerned with the observation, realization, analysis and application of the governing dynamics of every situation to understand the fine lines of energies at work, to take control of them or manipulate the influence of either energy polarity to our advantage. This applies to and concerns every aspect of human activity. Positive, negative or neutral-those are the governing dynamics of the strange divine fluctuation of energy and space we call –Life!

2. HUMAN BODY-

TARGETS & WEAPONS

The human body has numerous anatomical weak spots like organs, soft tissue, muscles, joints, ligaments and bones. The hardest bone structures are the skull and hip bone; the weakest are the throat, fingers, collarbone, ribcage and bones of the hands and feet. The most pressure sensitive spots are the eyes, throat and genitals. These can not be trained and toughened-therefore always present a target. The 5 major targets in any self defense situation are: eyes-throat-solar plexus-groin-knee cap- which are all attacked with strikes and kicks-aiming at neutralizing the attack and to finish the confrontation quickly.

The weapons one has at his/her disposal are the fingers, fists, palm, and edge of the hand, fore-arm, elbow, head, instep, knee, shin, sole and heel. The hands are used to trap, deflect, parry and strike-the legs to block, kick, stomp and move-placing one self thru footwork and evasive head and body moves in an advantageous position, while off-balancing the attacker. Knowing where to strike or kick with the right tool means maximizing ones chances of survival! Also reduces the chance of an uncontrolled violent outburst on the part of the defender, for reasons of damage control. As Martial Artists we do have the responsibility to avoid the misuse of the powers of our skills, harnessed in years of hard training. Don't break what you can toss or wrap!

Breaking bones and spilling blood means evidence for the courts and lawyers! It is also contradictive to the code of a spiritual warrior. The very ideogram of Wu-Shu or Budo-depicts a hand intercepting a weapon, meaning the art of stopping violence! Don't be a hypocrite and turn into what you seek to avoid or try to protect against! Be true to your self and your principles. Use your powers wisely! Enjoy life-protect it-don't waste or ruin it! That is the true meaning of Inyo Budo Taijutsu!

Violence erupts quickly, brutally and with an overwhelming rush of energy. The mind is blocked by the sudden outburst; therefore, the trained fighter will react in reflex, rather than freezing or flailing. Subconsciously stored responses take over; the mind leaves the body alone, which knows exactly what to do; that is the only surrender you should have in mind. Surrender to what is, to your body, to the flux of energies, not to your opponent, that would leave you at their mercy; surrender means don't resist- yield to overcome; that is the principle of BUDO, not force against force.

HUMAN BODY AND ITS WEAK POINTS

18 BASIC TARGETS

THE 5 PRIMARY TARGETS:

*Eyes

*Throat

*Solar Plexus

*Groin

*Kneecap

THE 13 SECONDARY TARGETS:

*Temple

*Ears

*Nose

*upper Lip (under Nose)

*Jaw

*Collarbone

* Ribcage

* Liver

*Kidney

*Bladder

*Bones

*Joints

*Achilles heel

HUMAN WEAPON

18 TOOLS OF COMBAT

Split into sections, the human body can be divided into a set of weapons, using the different limbs and body parts as differently shaped tools of attack and protection.

The hands and arms, legs and head serve as protective barrier as well as counter instruments to finish the aggressive encounter.

The fist, the fingers, the palm, the back of the hand, the ridge of the hand, the thumb, the knuckles, the bone of the forearm and elbow as well as the shoulder can be utilized to strike, block, parry and redirect any incoming attack or opening in defense. Attack and defense respond simultaneously, not in a common ½-strike/block-rhythm, which would put you at a disadvantage.

The shin, instep, toes, ball of the foot, the sole and the heel as well as the knee of course, can be used to kick, block, redirect any incoming lower region attack, such as kicks, takedown attempts, and counter attacks from within striking range.

The leg is longer and stronger than the arm, therefore a strike can be easily outreached and countered with a devastating kick to one of the in the previous chapter mentioned targets.

The head and skull is not just a target, but also a formidable close- range weapon. The head butt is a 360° technique-which means, it can be utilized in all directions, front, sides and to the rear, even up and down. Evading a strike to the head with footwork, evasive motions and body movements can amplify your counter, as well as keep you safe and out of trouble.

The whole body is used to work as ca single, dynamic, revolving unit, one move flawlessly and smoothly flowing into the next, moving in and out of range; striking, blocking, kicking and evading. Most important but way too often underestimated: correct and sufficient breathing! Especially for smokers: No breath-no life! One can protect himself blindfolded, but not breathless! Breathing regulates not only Ki and stamina, but also your emotional state of mind!

3. MOST COMMON ATTACKS

This section describes briefly the most common forms of attack, as it happens constantly all around the world. The assaults mentioned include the most common grabs, strikes, kicks and weapon attacks. In each of the following sections in this book, we will deal with every attack more in depth, according to the method or tool of response. The next examples merely denote the ways in which the average person is usually confronted in a violent encounter.

The most common attack forms involve either grabbing or pushing, a fist strike-usually aimed at the head or face, a kick aimed at the mid section or groin or legs, or a tackle with which the attacker is trying to knock the "victim" off-balance. Last common attacks involve the use of weapons, either makeshift as in simply grabbing any object within reach-or the use of blades, firearms and sticks. But never forget: violence creates even more violence! It is a self generating vicious circle, feeding on pain and problems! What we try to do here, is finding the right balance to effectively counter violent attacks, without becoming violent perpetrators ourselves. That means choosing your response wisely, even though they might be split-second decisions. That is what training and practice is for-to prepare you for worst case scenarios when your skills are in critical demand, so to speak. Now, the following examples are illustrating how the basic tools can be utilized to protect you from real life-violent assaults, outside the ring, without gloves, referee and eight counts. Where only your primal survival instincts can safe you...

The most common unarmed attacks can be divided into striking, kicking, grabbing, pushing and a combination of them. However there is also the possibility of multiple opponents attacking you in different ways at the same time. Just as you have several solutions of how to deal with them at your ready disposal. This section however, deals only with one on one-confrontations, as it is meant only as an introductory text and not as how to-manual.

Any responsible martial artist would advise at this point to seek professional instruction from a qualified expert, rather than trying to learn from reading books. The present author agrees to that wholeheartedly, based upon personal experience. Self-taught disarming methods can lead to fatal mistakes, therefore, a book like the one you are reading right now, can only show some possible solutions for critical situations, but not teach them!

Most common basic attacks:

The shortlist below contains some of the most common attacks and the following section briefly denotes possible basic solutions to deal with them:

* One/two hand push
* one/two hand chest grab
* punch to the face
* kick to groin/stomach
* one/two hand frontal/side choke
* naked rear choke
*1/2- leg tackle

One hand frontal choke/chest-grab/push

Press your chin onto your chest to protect your throat- grab hostile wrist and elbow and twist

Two hand push/grab/choke

Twist your hips to deflect/push hostile's arms up or down to dissolve/grab and counter with kick

Strikes to the

head

You can use your elbow and upper arm to protect from a strike to temple/chin/throat/neck

Kick to midsection/head

Block hostile kick or catch the leg to protect your temple/chin/throat/neck with both arms

Naked rear choke

Pull the choking arm with both hands off your throat and turn towards your opponent- counter

4. SELFDEFENSE GUIDELINES

*minimum effort- maximum protective efficiency

* Never underestimate any opponent!

* expect the unexpected!

* keep a low gravity center at all times!

* Limbs are kept close to the body to protect!

* Power comes from relaxation not tension!

* Never turn your back to your opponent!

* Always keep your vision peripheral!

* Leverage is stronger than muscle force!

* attack the 5 primary targets first

* attack 45°-protect 360°-off balance in 8 directions

* Never strike single hits; use doubles-

as well as revolving combinations!

* Initiative-interception-counter

(sen no sen-go no sen)

* use the 5 ways of attack in rapid fire motion!

* Never telegraph your movement –

unless it is a feint!

* strike –unbalance-lock-strike

* neutralize and finish attack instantly!

* 6 barriers protect head and body!

* Whole body involves in action!

(Kinetic linking)

5. FUNDAMENTAL MOVEMENTS

The purpose of the basic natural movements of forward-backward-left and right step is to bring you closer-further away or to the flank of any incoming attack or target-mobility of attack and protection. Combine the four corner steps and a half turn with the rear foot to either side to a single, smooth and mobile attacking-protecting-evading footwork and you have the basic building blocks.

Advance a single or double step to take the initiative or intercept your opponents move

Retreat a single step or two to adjust the range and counter

Left and right move help to evade any straight angle attack-open chance to counter to nearest target

Half turn to left and right using your hips to rotate-can redirect frontal attacks, off balance opponent and opens chance to counter attack from the side and rear

180° turn-north/south - getting out of an opponent's grab often requires a half or full body turn-even up to a full 360° spin, without losing balance-lower your center of gravity and keep your back straight-head down-eyes at the opponent-vision peripheral

There are also 5 ranges to be taken into account:

* Kicking   (from knee to tiptoes)

* Striking   (from elbow to fingertips)

* Trapping   (from shoulder to hand)

* Grappling   (from wrist to shoulder)

* Disarming   (from finger to shoulder)

6. BASIC UNARMED SELF PROTECTION

The following examples only illustrate possible basic solutions for some very common and perilous attacks, but are not meant as a crash-course Inyo Budo Taijutsu or street fighting. The concept of Inyo Taijutsu is designed to transcend the notion of martial arts and styles and their limiting labels, into energy and movement expressed thru the whole body, according to the situation.

Naked rear chokes escape

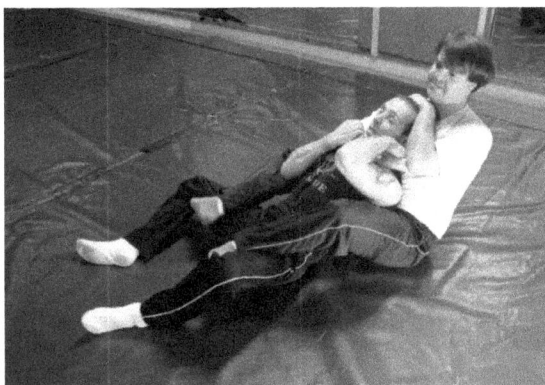

Ground sleeper choke with hooks

One of the most dangerous attacks is the sleeper or naked rear choke. It seals the larynx and the jugular vain and carotid artery on both sides of the neck, causing a quick knock out by preventing oxygen and blood flowing to the brain. There are two versions of the sleeper choke-standing and on the ground-each requires several different solutions.

Standing sleeper choke

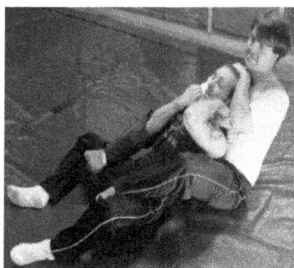

A

B

C

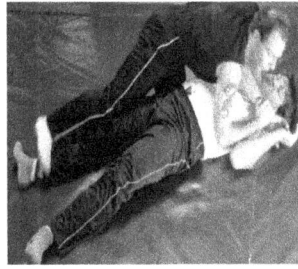

D

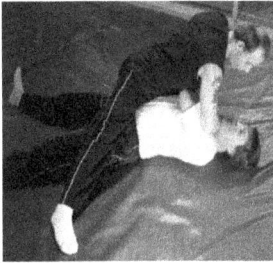

E

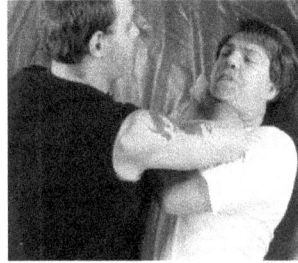

F

Escape from choke on the ground

A   Choked from behind, pull hostile arm down

B   twist your hips and move your leg over his

legs

C   control the arm and pass his guard to free
your self under his armpit

D   control hostile arm and leg with one hand

E   press forearm and elbow into hostile throat

F   close up on choke

A

B

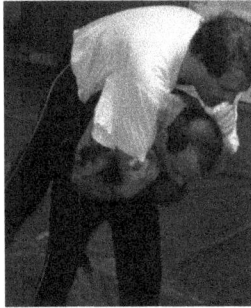

C

D

E

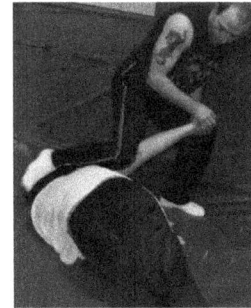

F

Escape from standing rear choke

A   Choked from behind, grab hostiles wrist

        and arm

B   press your chin in his arm crook and bend

        forward

C   pull his arm off your throat and down, bend

        your knees

D   push hard back with your hips

        and stretch your legs out

E   hostile crashlands, control

        his arm at wrist and elbow

F   press your knee onto his elbow

        and push down.

A

B

C

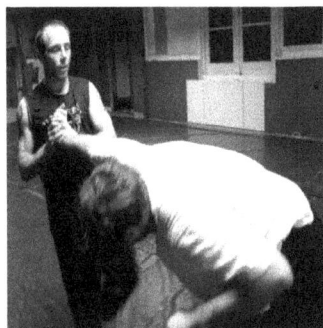

D

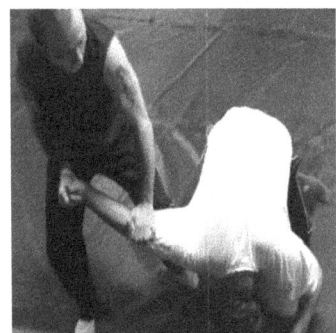

E

F

Against one hand frontal choke

A   grabbed by the throat-press your chin

between hostiles thumb and index finger

B   grab his wrist and twist it clockwise

C   grab with two hands - twist and kick to

the stomach or groin

D   apply reverse wristlock with two hands

E   apply with one hand pressure to the

elbow and press Hostile down

F   hold wristlock with both hands and

finish with kick to the ribs

A

B

C

D

E

F

45

Against strike to the head

A   strike to the head is evaded

B   parry the arm and push it to create space

C   get behind hostile-grab his waist and
          neck and pull him off balance

D   press your knee into the back of his
          knee and take him down

E   wrap your arms around his throat and
          body control hostile-pulling him back

F   squeeze elbows-finish with sleeper choke

A

B

C

D

E

F

Against strike to the head - variation

A   squaring off-raise your guard

B   parry strike and come forward

C   strike to the chin or throat

D   step forward and bend his

        arm with under hook

E   shoot knee strike to the ribs or

        liver – lever his arm and pull down

F   pull hostile down and finish with

        strikes or joint lock

A

B

C

D

Against strike to the head - variation

A   strike is deflected-

B   counter with palm strike to chin-

         push head back to off-balance hostile

C   place your foot behind his-bend and

         lever his arm with two hands

D   pull his arm down and press your leg

         into hostiles knee to off-balance him

E   turn your hips and take hostile

         down on his back

F   finish with elbow pressured-wristlock

A

B

C

D

E

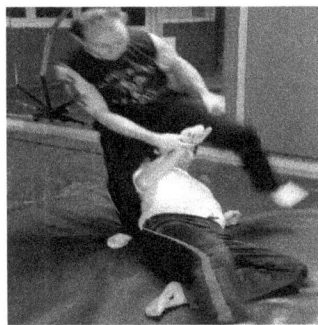

F

Against strike and kick- variation

A   parry incoming strike to the inside

B   sidestep front kick attempt

C   grab hostiles waist and bypass him

D   get behind hostile-grab his neck and arm

E   pull hostile down on his back-secured

        by a throat hold and under hook

F   control hostiles arm and finish with

        Kicks to the head and body

A

B

C

D

E

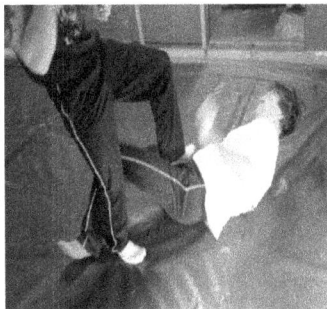

F

53

Against strike and kick- variation

A   strike is deflected and evaded,

B   kick attempt is parried with leg-block

C   counter with straight lead punch

D   knock hostile down with cross-palm strike

E   strike hostile in the guts and groin

F   finish with groin and body kicks

A

B

C

D

E

F

Against strike/grab/push to the head /throat

A   grab or strike is deflected

B   press hostiles arm down to create opening

C   counter with hook strike to the chin

D   followed up with a knee to the body

E   grab hostiles neck and apply pressure to the throat and neck-controlling his arm

F   Take hostile down-finish with choke hold

7. TAIJUTSU vs. ARMED ATTACK

Fighting unarmed opponents is one thing-facing deadly weapons like a gun or blade something entirely different-now the danger is as real as it gets. One mistake might very well be your last one. A knife is most dangerous from close by - a gun from further away. Within the length of your arm, you have at least a 50/50 chance to redirect or disarm the gun threat. Thereby form the barrel and its opening obviously the biggest danger.

A knife poses an even greater hazard. Due to its size and the fact that it can be easily hidden and in an instant deployed, with the razor-sharp cutting edge, and the pointed tip. This makes any blade a formidable and deadly weapon. Designed to cut skin, tendons and veins and penetrate flesh and organs like a miniature sword, it can be double edged, ragged, curved, razor like or even as long as a machete. It can be used to cut, slash, pierce, and even been thrown into its target.

It is always important to protect head and body from the fire line as well as the legs from the stabbing and cutting range, which is at least as far as one and a half arm lengths. Better to avoid worst case scenarios than being a dead hero.

The following examples illustrate some possible solutions for worst case scenarios, dealing with knife and gun threats; but again - are not meant as crash course disarming.

Weapon disarming is no horse play but might mean the ultimate difference between life and death. Not to be taken lightly, especially when practicing with life- blades or ammo, or in the safe environment of a trainings hall. Can easily be misleading into fatality!

GUN REDIRECTING & DISARMING

Frontal gun threat

A

B

C

D

E

F

Against gun threat from the front

A   twist your hips and quickly push the
gun away from your body

B   grab the barrel and hostiles wrist with
both hands

C   twist the wrist and gun towards hostile

D   press down and lever the wrist and
Elbow-gun pointing to the ground

E   kick hostile in the face or body to push
him back and disarm him

F   control hostile at gun point

A

B

C

D

E

F

Against gun threat from the front-variation

A twist your hips and deflect frontal gun threat

B grab the barrel, twist and pull towards hostile

C support your arm by slipping your other

arm underneath the hostiles wrist

D step forward and pull hostiles arm

down- applying full body leverage

E take hostile down, while controlling his

arm and gun-pointing at hostiles head

F control hostile with both hands at gun point

A

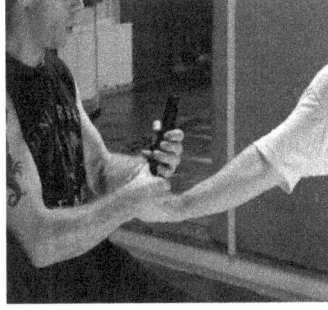

B

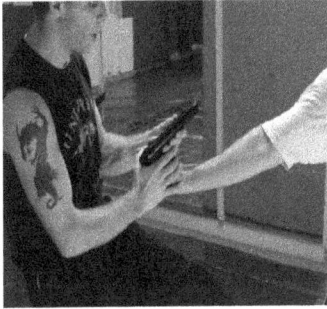

C

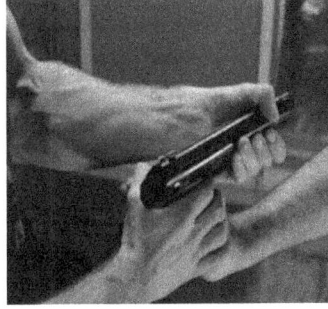

D

E

F

Against gun threat from the side

A   step back-deflect gun threat with one hand

B   grab barrel and wrist with both hands-

          twist towards hostile to break the grip

C   change your grip on the barrel and apply

          down ward pressure on hostiles wrist

D   grab the barrel firmly and pull back

E   pull back and press hostiles wrist

          down – firmly securing the gun

F   apply leverage and control hostile with

          wrist lock takedown at gun point

A

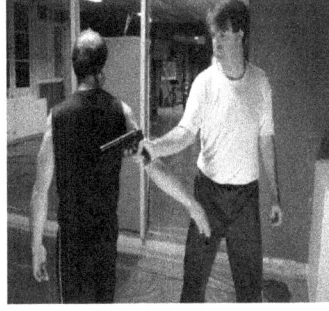

B

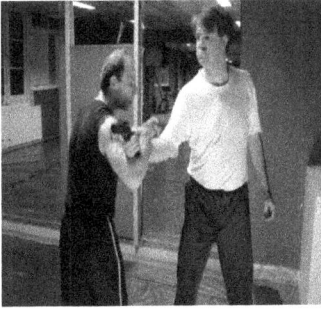

C

D

E

F

Against gun threat from the rear

A   gun in your back-turn clockwise to avoid
line of fire

B   use your momentum and deflect the gun
with your arm

C   lock the gun arm tight in your biceps crook

D   smack hostile with an elbow strike and
redirect the gun at his wrist

E   twist the gun towards hostile and push

F   apply leverage to the wrist and force
Hostile at gunpoint on his knees

A

B

C

D

E

F

Against gun threat from the rear-variation

A   Gun in the back-twist counter clockwise

B   turn your hips and deflect the gun to the

Outside of your body

C   lock the gun arm tight with under hook

D   smack hostile with a back fist in the face

E   follow up with a edge hand strike to the

throat and if you want-sweep his foot

F   control the gun arm and press hostile

down – with leverage to the chin

A

B

C

D

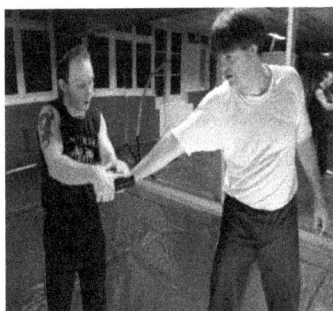

E

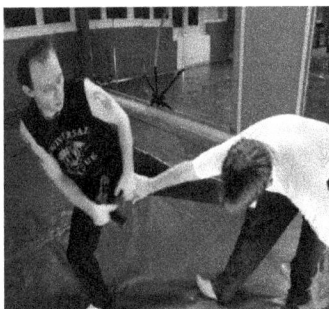

F

Against frontal gun threat to the head

A   gun at your forehead

B   turn your hips to leave line of fire

C   grab the barrel with two hands

D   twist the gun towards hostile

E   twist the gun while levering hostiles

           wrist – Pulling it sideways off his grip

F   control gun hand and side kick

           Hostile's Body or legs to disarm him

KNIFE REDIRECTING & DISARMING

Whereas a gun usually poses a threat from the 4 corners, front back and sides, to the head and midsection, close by and far away; a knife can be wielded in close and middle range in multiple ways from every angle.

There are a number of different ways to hold a knife, various cuts, slashes and ways to stab, pierce and combine cuts and stabs in rapid fire succession, much

like bullets coming out of a semi-automatic firearm. The whole body is from top to toe a living, breathing, bleeding, moving target! Most traditional martial arts or basic self defense courses focus on primary cuts and stabs to head and torso, neglecting the vital areas on the legs, like the femur artery. It is most important to know the venomous speed and various ways, in which a blade can be utilized. What areas are most likely to be attacked, which the hardest targets to protect and how to avoid getting cut or stabbed. Avoidance is much better than healing!

But for those worst case scenarios, where avoidance failed, escape is impossible and fighting for your life becomes a shocking reality, quick, decisive counter attacks to neutralize and redirect or disarm the knife attack are the last resort to turn to. When attacked by a knife wielding maniac, don't go at it barehanded, unless you know exactly what you are doing. Again, there is no need to become a dead hero!

Use common objects in your immediate environment as weapons to shield, distract or counter. This can be anything from rolling up your jacket into a protective cushion, some hairspray used as maze, a chair, umbrella, hot liquid, or even a parked bicycle for that matter. Whatever you find to protect yourself – use it. Survival is the key!

The following examples show unarmed disarming methods, which are advised not to be practiced without professional supervision! Don't rely in critical situations on things you have read in a book! Never underestimate the ultimate danger of that sharp edged bladed weapon! Be smart-survive!

A

B

C

D

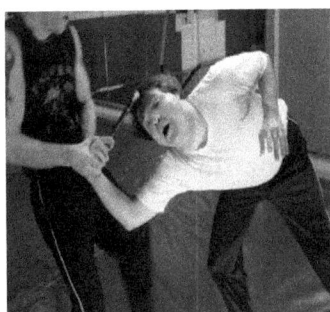

E

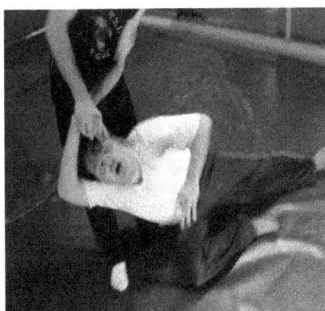

F

Against frontal knife threat-stab

A   stab to the stomach is blocked to the outside

B   grab knife hand by the wrist with two hands

C   twist the hostile wrist counter clockwise

D   kick to the groin or ribs to off balance hostile

E   pull hostile to you –press the wrist down

F   press down and disarm hostile to the ground

A

B

C

D

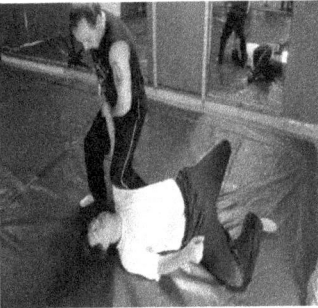

E

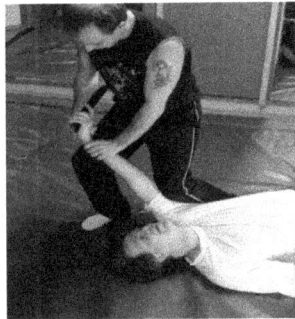

F

Against frontal knife attack-slash

A slash from the outside is thwarted at the wrist

B grab wrist and palm strike to hostiles chin

C place your foot behind his and off balance
Hostile with heel sweep

D push his head back and sweep the foot-
At the same time control the knife arm

E control his knife arm with leg pressure
and apply Leverage at the elbow

F control and disarm the knife hand

A

B

C

D

E

F

Against frontal slash - variation

A   Knife slash from above

B   over head deflect at the wrist

C   deflect the knife arm downward and

punch hostile with a hook on the chin

D   pull the knife arm down and

off balance hostile

E   strike down on hostile's biceps crook-

bend his arm and apply elbow lock

F   control hostile on the ground - press

the knife in his grip against his throat

A

B

C

D

E

F

Against frontal slash - variation

A   downward slash is anticipated

B   deflect strike with overhead parry

C   grab knife hand at the wrist and strike
     Hostile's liver or kidney

D   pull the knife arm firmly down and
     off - balance hostile

E   press down on hostiles shoulder

F   Finish with arm bar takedown

A

B

C

D

E

F

Against frontal slash - variation

A   deflect downward slash with

Overhead parry

B   step forward and palm strike to the chin

C   pull knife arm- strike the chin and

Sweep Hostiles foot

D   press hostiles face down; apply

leverage to the knife arms elbow

E   press your leg onto hostiles chest-

While pressing his face down

F   control hostile on the ground

and disarm him with leg-arm bar

A

B

C

D

E

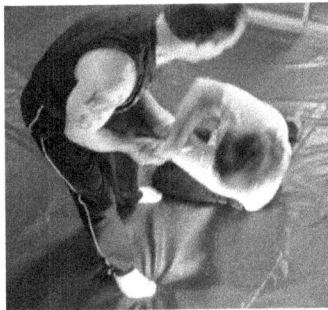

F

Against rear knife attack-throat cut

A rear knife threat on the throat

B grab the knife hand at the wrist and pull it down-away from your throat

C turn your hips while firmly controlling the knife hand

D step back and turn 180° counter clockwise-Redirecting the blade towards hostile

E apply leverage to hostiles elbow and force him down on his knees

F control hostile on the ground at knife point

8. Aftermath

This modest volume represents the 3rd and final basic introduction manual of the Inyo Budo & Taijutsu concept, which is not a formal martial art, but conveys the idea of transcending the notion of styles into energy and movement, training and using the whole body for the purpose of fitness and self protection.

The yin yang dynamics of antagonism, support and balance are the key to the primary philosophical perspective, in all aspects of life. The art of becoming and being master or champion of your life! The motto is fitness-self-protection and personal development-to lead a more efficient, healthier and happier life!

The real highest excellence in martial art and human development is not destruction and murder - it is the art of learning and healing! Also to heal one self spiritually from old wrongs, emotional pain, traumas, phobias, ego-tripping etc. The only constant in life as we know, is change.

That is the core principle of yin and yang. To resist those changes causes internal and external turmoil.

To come to a higher level of consciousness, the spiritual aspects of meditation and Qi Gong are necessary tools on your behalf. The yin yang (in yo in Japanese) concept was designed by the ancient Taoists to help us understand the universal principles and adjust easier to the dynamics and changes in life.

Self protection starts with ones attitude and awareness. Physical responses such as techniques and combat moves are only labels, clouding real understanding and spontaneous expression of oneself in any given situation. Martial and spiritual arts are supposed vehicles on your life-path, not obstructions. It only becomes a burden when the ego creates labels, limitations and dogmatic views, clinging to artificial rituals, obsolete traditions or hostile jealousy for fear of exposure. This only creates madness and conflicts!

The real purpose of Inyo Budo & Taijutsu is to help to protect you physically on your way and to come spiritually to a deeper understanding of your own true nature. Not to create more violence thru aggressive behavior and efficient combat-moves.

Mudo Nandayo HEISEI XXII

About the author

Mudo Nandayo (*1973); certified life-coach, fitness & knife combat instructor; former student and instructor at the legendary Vos Gym Amsterdam, advocate of the Inyo Budo - Governing Dynamics of self protection and self improvement-concept, recently left his 2nd home-Vos Gym after a decade and retired after 25 years from the martial arts world after recovering from a series of injuries and a massive burn-out. Due to a severe case of post-traumatic stress disorder no longer teaches, committing himself fulltime to his family, practicing and writing.

OTHER TITLES BY MUDO NANDAYO:

INYO BUDO-GOVERNING DYNAMICS   © 2011

The original basic introduction textbook of the Governing Dynamics concept-revised edition

THE ART OF BEING CHAMPION OF YOUR LIFE © 2011

Basic Guidebook on how to use the benefits of the spiritual and martial arts to improve oneself and master a more efficient, healthy and successful life

MUSHA SHUGYO-WARRIOR'S QUEST © 2011

The principal theory and philosophy of Inyo Budo & Taijutsu and how to transmit them pragmatically

In progress: MASTERS OF 20TH CENTURY © 2011

LEGENDS OF THE NINJA © 2011

WARLORDS AND WARRIORS © 2011

SECRET OF DRUNKEN BOXING © 2011

www.ingramcontent.com/pod-product-compliance
Lightning Source LLC
Chambersburg PA
CBHW071017040426

42443CB00007B/825

*9 7 8 1 1 0 5 2 4 8 8 4 9 *